HERE'S WHAT PEOPLE ARE SAYING ABOUT
AFTER THE SPEECH, WHEN TEENS GET REAL

"*After The Speech, When Teens Get Real* is an honest look into how teens feel and the challenges they face. It's a great read where every story offers guidance and tools on how to face fears, take action to overcome challenges, and live a healthy, balanced life."

—Christine Hassler, Keynote Speaker,
Author of *Expectation Hangover*

"Harriet does what she was put on earth to do, both on and off stage. From the opening story, I was hooked. Her compassion, wisdom, and genuine heart for each person she interacts with jumps off the page."

—Ray Lozano, CEO,
Prevention Plus

"The stories that Harriet recalls throughout this book will cause you to be very purposeful and attentive when speaking to a teenager. It opens your eyes to the reality of how the trials of life affect teens. The transparency that is exchanged between Harriet and her teenage audience is amazing. These stories highlight how one person can spend a limited time with a young person and change his or her life forever. Harriet Turk is not only a public speaker; she is a champion, advocate, and life saver to her teenage audiences. Wow!"

—Joy Bivens, School Board Member,
Whitehall City Schools, Ohio

D1368407

"*After the Speech, When Teens Get Real* is the kind of book that will inspire readers of all ages and backgrounds. It's poignant, raw, and heartening stories take readers on a journey that reminds us of both the wonder of resilience and the power of human connection."

>—Sophie Brickman, BA in Psychology and
>Health: Science, Society, and Policy,
>Brandeis University

"Every summer, Youth to Youth International utilizes national speakers that inspire and engage young people at our summer training conferences. We look for speakers who are down to earth, relatable to teens, honest on the stage and off, and genuinely care about students beyond their job at hand. Harriet Turk is one of the BEST! She continuously works at her craft, keeping her material relevant and approachable."

>—Jill Smock, Director,
>Youth to Youth International

"Harriet is passionate about encouraging teens to live their dreams, passionate about her message of youth empowerment, and passionate in her desire to help teens gain the skills to better themselves. She has the ability to forge a strong connection with her teen audience."

>—Jack Foster, Former Program Coordinator,
>Aroostook Teen Leadership Camp Program

After the Speech

When Teens Get Real

Harriet Turk

Copyright © 2016 Harriet Turk

All rights reserved.

Names have been changed to protect the privacy of individuals.

ISBN: 978-1530129911

For Andrew

CONTENTS

ACKNOWLEDGMENTS

Clayton Shelvin, you gave me the idea for this book. I can't thank you enough.

My business might not be alive today had it not been for fellow speaker and friend, Scott Backovich. Thank you for helping me rekindle my enthusiasm for my career. Without your friendship, I'm not sure I would still be a professional speaker today. You are forever a part of my family.

Thank you to my son, Andrew, who has never had his mom at home like most moms are and who tells me he's used to me being gone so it's "no big deal." You'll never know how much I love my work and how much I dread leaving you.

Thank you to my editor, Kathleen Shryock, who can figure out what I want to say like no one else has ever been able to. How she can do this when we have never met in person is a true mystery. Thanks for all you do.

Finally, thanks to all the students who approached me after one of my programs. The opportunities to shake a hand, give you a hug, take a picture with you, or just have a quick conversation mean so much to me. In all of these ways, you let me know that the time I spent with you mattered.

To the students who asked for my autograph so you could sell it on eBay, I apologize. I'm sure you didn't make a dime. In my defense, I did try to warn you.

PROLOGUE

I usually catch them out of the corner of my eye.

They hang back—away from the crowd that surrounds me—and try hard for me not to notice them. But that's when I start to watch them, because I know they are the ones who really need to talk to me. Before I can get to them, I'm surrounded by other, more assertive students who want to take a picture with me, to pick up one of my chant cards, or who just want to tell me, "I think you'd be a cool mom!"

I love talking with the first group that rushes in, but I don't want those other students to leave, and I'm scared they will. In those in-between moments when they have time to think about what they want to tell me, their nerves might take over and they might head for the door. In the past, I've watched them give up and leave.

And then I either don't know how to find them, or I can't stay long enough and they are gone forever.

That breaks my heart.

Audiences believe that the standing ovation marks the end of the presentation. They assume that once the speech is over, it's time to go. That's not even close—at least, not for me. The time immediately following the formal presentation is a new beginning. That's when my audience expresses their transparent hearts. That's when their masks come off. That's when it gets personal.

I listen to their stories. I watch their eyes. I hear the emotion in their voices. And I observe their body language. Sometimes, the stories are fun and we laugh. But there are many times when the stories resonate how I felt as a teen: unsure of myself, unworthy, confused, fat, fabulous, and depressed, all at the same time.

More often than not, these young people are quickly satisfied by a penetrating dose of my life's lessons; timely tales that can transform what was an insurmountable issue a few minutes before into a problem that can be solved with sensible advice and a smile.

It is the remaining kids—the ones waiting on the sidelines—who aren't so easy to counsel. Their issues are gut-wrenching, even heartbreaking; and either I don't know how to help, or I'm actually shocked that yet another teen has to endure such a horrible home life, unbearable confusion, abusive relationship, bullying, or a fake friend that has led them down the wrong path.

In a quick, few minutes, they've come to me for help. Sometimes, I can. Sometimes, I can't. And sometimes, they leave before I get the chance. I don't want to help some of my audience. I want to be there for all of them.

After the Speech, When Teens Get Real is an entertaining and poignant collection of true stories from young people who have reached out to me as I have traveled the country. I was lucky enough to meet some of them in person. A few I know only through the note that was pressed in my hand while I was talking with someone else. Others have contacted me through a personal phone call, email, Facebook message, or letter. I've kept in contact with some of them for years, and others I knew only for a minute. And some of them were those tentative students who were waiting in the wings, longing to share their stories with someone who has been there and needing to believe in the promise of a better future.

They have all made an impression on me, and I thought it was time for you to meet them, too. I hope that you will be as inspired by their stories as I am because everyone needs to believe in their future, especially teenagers.

Fasten your seat belt. You are about to meet some wonderful people with the courage to keep fighting for their dreams.

It's not just about dreams; it's about life.

Harriet's Heart

You need to know that no matter what
you are going through at the moment,
a hopeful future filled with success
and happiness is waiting if you can
just hang in there.

CHAPTER ONE

HANG IN THERE!

"My mom is drunk all the time, my dad is in jail, and my grandfather who raises me has just been diagnosed with stage four cancer. He will die soon. I have to take care of my little sister, and I can't be a real teenager. I can't ever have fun, and I am always sad. What am I going to do when my grandfather dies? He's the only one who shows me any love," said Nick.

The words came pouring out of 15-year-old Nick's mouth as his eyes filled with tears. I stood there, stunned. This was a kid who had looked down at the floor during the entire assembly. I had assumed that he was bored out of his mind. The few times that he had looked at me, it was with contempt. Now, I understood why.

As I led the audience in an affirming, "Life IS

Great!" chant, he probably thought I had lost my mind. What part of his current life experience was great? No part.

It's at times like these when my job is really hard. I *do* believe that life is great. I *do* believe that we have to find positive moments, even in the darkest times. But how do you explain this philosophy to a fifteen-year-old who isn't allowed to be a teenager?

Adults in Nick's life expected him to be mature enough to live the after-school hours of his day as a nurse, father figure, adult, and caretaker. He was in an impossible situation. I knew that something had to change in order for him to have a chance.

I couldn't give him all of the answers he needed to hear in just a few minutes. This young man wasn't in control of his life. All he could do was grit his teeth day after day and get through it. I started by asking Nick a few questions. "Are there any adults besides your grandfather who you feel safe with? Is there a teacher or a coach at school who you think could help you with this?"

He named a few adults, including a teacher at the school. I immediately said, "Great. Let's go find her and tell her what's going on."

Nick started to resist and protested that he only wanted me to understand his situation. I turned to him and said, "As much as I'd love to help you, I'm only here at school for less than two hours. We need to find someone who can be here for you throughout the year, okay?"

He numbly nodded. He was so beaten down that I doubt he even believed me. I was being honest. I didn't know his school, his community, his city, or even his state. I couldn't help him with his support systems, because I didn't know them. I could suggest some generic things for him to do, but I didn't think he was in a position to take care of himself. He had been taking care of so many others. It was time for someone to take care of him.

At that point, Nick became concerned. He was supposed to be in English class. This was one area where I knew I could help him. I was the guest speaker and with that came a special privilege of being able to ask for things I wanted. At that moment, I wanted to help him, and if that meant he had to miss a class, so be it. What bothered me most was that he was more worried about what this teacher would think of him than about getting the help he so desperately needed. Nick was afraid that she would perceive him as a bad person instead of understanding that he was living in a bad situation. This young man was barely hanging on, but he believed that his anxious feelings were a reflection of who he was as a person and not a symptom of what he was going through. Nick was a sweet guy who didn't realize his personal value. I understood how he felt.

There are so many of us who take on other people's problems and make them our own. We begin to believe that we have to fix everyone else, and if we can't, then we aren't valuable.

That is false thinking. When we subscribe to false thinking, we bottle everything up inside and work hard to keep it together. We get overwhelmed and stressed out. As a result, the person we are trying to help might get what they want out of the situation, but we become exhausted and frustrated.

How can we be strong for those who need us if we

are too weak to help them? We have to remain emotionally healthy, and we can't do that when we are concentrating on everyone else but ignoring our own wellbeing!

Exhibiting the drive and dedication to assist others is awesome, and our desire to help is fueled by the very best intentions. The problem occurs when our focus denies us the ability to care for ourselves. Doing too much, and suffering as a result, is not healthy. Sometimes, we need to let go of things that are weighing us down.

Stop. Let it go. Sing the song from *Frozen* if you must. Let. It. Go.

Nick and I made it to the office of a teacher he trusted, and as luck would have it, it was during her planning period. The three of us sat down and talked. I explained to her that we wanted to talk about ways to bring some relief to Nick's life. The teacher and I suggested ideas and resources. The best part was that the she reassured him that her door was always open and that she would continue to make sure he had help. Then, Nick did something that made my heart leap for joy.

He smiled. Good, good, good!

I walked away knowing that, while nothing had changed concerning Nick's situation at home, the teacher and I had transformed his feelings of helplessness into hope. He had someone standing by his side. It was a start. By revealing his situation and discussing it, Nick learned that someone could help him get through a tough time.

Step one for successfully dealing with a tough situation is to share your concerns with a trusted friend or adult. No one can help if you keep everything inside. Establishing connections with resources and trusted adults can only occur when you put aside your fears and ask for help.

Repeat after me. "I will not take on other people's problems, and I will not believe that I have to fix them all. I have to take care of myself. My life matters, too."

Harriet's Heart

Even though you may feel like no one understands what you are going through, there is someone who does.

Don't close yourself off from the world.

Reach out and ask for help.

Reflections

- What steps can you take to adopt a "Life Is Great" attitude even when your life feels overwhelming and not so great?

- Do you have a trusted adult to turn to when you need help?

- Why is it important to take care of ourselves and not ignore our own needs?

CHAPTER TWO

A LETTER FOR MOM

Hi Harriet,

I saw you speak at a leadership conference in 2012. You do not remember me, but I sure remember you!

Your speech has stuck with me these past years, and I've recommended some of your YouTube videos to friends who have been going through difficult times as a means of feeling inspired and positive about their lives.

Lately, my mom has been going through some hard times in her personal life. Things have happened between her and my dad, her friends, colleagues and others, that have caused her to be stressed out. These things have made her feel down more than I would like.

There is a lot going on in our lives (financially, medically, etc.) and she feels all of it. She could use a bit of encouragement and inspiration, beyond what my sister and I try to do, to feel more positive about her life.

My mom will be returning to school this year (after 36 years) to slowly start the process of earning an associate's degree in English. She is looking forward to the challenge, and I am hoping it will allow her to focus her energy on something positive rather than all of the negatives that have hit her life over the last three to five years.

To clarify, I know there are people in worse situations. But all the little things add up, and my mom has felt the pressure from those things.

I guess what I am asking—and I'm sure you get a lot of similar requests—is if you could send a little note of encouragement to her and some messages that helped you feel inspired to change your life for the better?

I think hearing it from someone like you might inspire her to feel more positive and to change her attitude about some things in her life.

Your friend,
Lauren

Wow! Lauren's letter really touched my heart. I didn't specifically know what this incredible mom was going through, but I completely understood her feelings of being overwhelmed and out of control.

Sometimes, it's hard having a job as a motivational speaker because people assume that I walk around with my life in complete order and that each day is a big ball of sunshine. That couldn't be further from the truth. My life can be completely dysfunctional and chaotic. Sometimes, I am fabulous at providing guidance but terrible about taking my own advice.

I remember sitting at my computer, watching the

bids roll in for a place setting of china I was selling on eBay. I was excited because there was an online bidding war going on and the price was much higher than I had hoped. There were only 34 minutes left until the bidding closed, and the price was still climbing. I'd already sold 11 other place settings, and this was the last one. I couldn't believe it. The winning bid was going to far exceed my expectations. I was not only celebrating my good fortune; I was fighting for my financial life.

I was trying to take care of my toddler son, and I was doing everything I could to make sure he felt safe and secure. In short, I was a mess. Thirty minutes remained in the online auction, but I didn't have time to watch the final bids. I had to shut down my computer, walk purposefully out of my hotel room, and try to instill hope in others even though my own heart was heavy. I wondered if I had the right words to move my audience.

Across the street, 2,000 people were waiting for me in the convention center ballroom. That was a whole lot of folks who were expecting me to guide them toward the creation of a wonderful, hope-filled life. I hoped that I could convey my message in an engaging way. My agenda even included an action plan to help guide my audience members on their new journeys. I believed in my message. That group would never know that I was in the process of selling my china because I had only a few days to make a house payment, and I had no money.

Denial of the truth, blind faith, and a trusting heart were all realities that had led me to this place where my life was falling apart and I couldn't pay my bills. I was alone with my two-year-old son, and I didn't know what else to do but sell items from my attic. Thankfully, the china sets sold. I made it through the following month. And the advice and lessons I was giving to my audience felt like renewed words of wisdom. I wasn't just speaking to the crowd; I was also speaking to myself.

Life can be tough. Life can be hard. Sometimes, we feel overwhelmed. Sometimes, we need someone to let us know it's going to be all right. It may not be okay today or tomorrow, but one day, if we keep trying, it will be. We may have to give up on a situation, but we never have to give up on ourselves.

Of course I sent a message of encouragement to Lauren's mom. It wasn't just a nugget of wisdom; it came from the deepest part of me. I knew exactly how she was feeling.

Survival. . .even when it's tough. That's what you do. It's called living.

Harriet's Heart

Encouragement from others may be

just the thing to

help you make it through the day.

It might be the only spark you need to

reignite your dreams.

Reflections

- Have you ever experienced a time when you felt like your life was out of control or you just felt like giving up?

- If so, was it hard to give encouragement to others or to acknowledge anything good in your life?

- When you give encouragement to others, even when you aren't feeling so great about situations in your own life, do you start to feel better, too?

CHAPTER THREE

WHEN YOU'RE HOT, YOU'RE HOT!

As soon as I answered the phone, I heard the giggles. I was pretty sure I knew what was coming next. Yep. In unison, several voices started reciting the chant that I use during my presentations. It's the one that every audience member is encouraged to shout out by the end of my program:

> **"I AM somebody special. If you don't like me,**
> **TOUGH!**
> **'Cuz I am...cool enough...smooth enough...**
> **and doggone it...**
> **I am HOT enough to be who I want to be!"**

On these occasions, after my mystery callers get through the entire, laughter-filled message, they hang up. There's no interaction—no response from me—

except for the huge smile on my face.

I'm never sure why they call, but I'm glad they do. It lets me know they listened and they remember a part of my program. And for some reason, they want me to hear them. I especially love the part when they say, "I am HOT enough." Sometimes, they start making a sizzling sound to punctuate this point. I know they understand the meaning of this key phrase, because during the presentation, I thoroughly explain what I mean. I don't mean *hot* as in an outward, sexy look. I mean *hot* as in a confident, "I've got it going on" look. Out of the entire chant, that's the most important part, because no matter what anyone says, they all do have IT!

We all have the IT factor, that special something that makes us unique and helps to define us. But so many times, we hide it and don't let people see our authentic selves. We don't let others hear us sizzle. When we actually allow ourselves to be hot and really let it rip, that is when we have the most fun. That is when we really live.

HOT. The students understand what I mean. They were there when I said it and explained it. They embrace it. But every few months, I get a call from a parent who found the chant card that looks like a business card on one side and includes the chant on the opposite side. They randomly discovered it in their child's room or in a backpack, and they wonder, "Where in the world did this come from? Why is someone teaching my child to be HOT?"

These parents aren't giggling on the phone, and their tone is anything but happy. The conversation usually begins with a curt, "I found this card in my child's room, and I want to know if you gave it to her and what is this HOT stuff all about?"

I explain, "It's a chant I use in my programs, and I give the card to students who would like one." I know what's coming next.

"We teach our children not to concentrate on their outward appearances, and we certainly don't want them walking around and boasting about being hot! That is definitely not what we want our child to focus on, and this teaches the direct opposite of that."

I politely explain the meaning of hot and why I think it's important for young people to feel this way. I clarify that I'm not in any way, shape, or form, telling students to act sexy or to concentrate on their physical looks. Instead, being hot involves a focus on inner beauty and self-confidence. Usually, I win the parents over. Sometimes, they remain skeptical.

Regardless of their response, I always end the call the same way. "Would you please ask your child about the meaning of the card when he or she comes home? If your child's explanation doesn't match what I told you, call me back. I'll talk to your child some more. I'll do a better job of getting my point across so that he or she understands. We can complete the call on speaker phone so that you both can hear exactly what I am saying."

I've never had a parent call me back. But these communications always make me wonder, "Why didn't these parents talk with their children first, before calling me? They were obviously concerned about their child, so why didn't they approach their child?"

Healthy communication between a parent and teenager is vital. When we don't have that, we can lose sight of what is really happening. We make assumptions without taking the time to learn the truth. The end result is a chipping away at the important relationships between parents and their children. We might even stop trusting one another.

Many parents are fond of saying, "I'm not your friend; I'm your parent." When I was growing up, I'm not sure how many times I heard that familiar phrase, but it was enough for me to get the message. It was even enough for me to believe that I couldn't openly share things with my parents.

The interesting thing is that by the time kids are teenagers, most of them feel the same way that I did. They have heard this message enough to know that their parents are not their friends. In reality, it's a time when most teenagers are more comfortable sharing their secrets and problems with friends, instead of their parents or other key adults. The parent has been the authority figure throughout the child's life. Adolescence is difficult to navigate, and teenagers would rather chart their own course alongside their peers than float under the direction of someone who has served as their ship's captain. So we are left with a situation in which parents and children don't talk, not even about their concerns. And that's a problem. We need to communicate. We need to trust.

Parents have been conditioned not to be "friends" with their children, and they do have an important role to play beyond any friendship. After all, parents have already navigated the rough waters of adolescence. They know it's not easy, and they want their children to be safe and happy. It's their job to set boundaries. But that doesn't mean that parents can't have friendly conversations with their teens. And it doesn't mean that teens can't have friendly conversations with their parents.

So take the first step. Share something new with your parents or the trusted adults in your life. Ask them what they would have done in high school when faced with a certain situation. Find out what they were interested in and what challenges they faced. You may be surprised to learn that your parents understand more than you think they do. When your parents get upset or freak out, it may be because they have suffered through something similar and they don't want you to get hurt.

Your parents may never be your best friends. That's okay. But while friends come and go, your parents will be the ones to help you pick up the pieces and keep going.

Trust me. I'm a mom. I know these things.

Harriet's Heart

Look at the possibilities.

A possibility is all you need to get

started.

Reflections

- We all have an "IT" factor. What's yours?

- When you do allow yourself to "sizzle" (and are free to be you), how do you feel?

- Do you believe you can talk freely to your parents/guardians? What would improve your communication with your parents/guardians?

CHAPTER FOUR

BE TRUE TO YOU

Hello Harriet,

I met you at the state convention. My name is Thomas, aka Mr. Happy Pants. I was the one who came up to you at the end of your workshop and told you that I could relate to your keynote presentation. I would like to go into depth about what I was trying to say.

I didn't realize I was like this until you said something that really made me think about who I am. I realized that I have a different personality for every group I hang out with. I don't know how to change that and just be me.

I was hoping that you could give me tips on how I can do that. I'm a huge people pleaser, and I feel like I need everyone to like me. I have had some tough days in my life so far. My parents divorced, our house was foreclosed on, and I am now living in a one bedroom apartment with three people. I experienced abandonment from my father because of his hardcore drug use, and this year, my mother was diagnosed with stage four colon cancer and was given a few years to live.

I still manage to keep a smile on my face, because that's what I've been told to do as a leader. I want my smile to have a domino effect beginning with me and extending out to others around me. But now, I realize how fake that makes me.

I really need tips on how to be genuine so that everyone will know the real Thomas. I've seen/heard a lot of keynote speakers but none as eye opening as you. God bless you, and I hope to hear from you soon.

Sincerely,
Thomas

P.S. My dream is to become a motivational speaker.

Sometimes, a letter from a young person really touches my soul. As I read Thomas' letter, I realized that I was holding my breath. What a courageous young man. I knew that I had to respond right away, and I wanted to find just the right words that would address Thomas' concerns but also validate his strength in facing such difficult circumstances.

Dear Thomas,

Wow! What a load you have had to deal with. How ironic that you have won the title of Mr. Happy Pants.

First, I'm so sorry about your mom's illness. In a very small way, I can relate to your pain. One of my very best friends is in remission from ovarian cancer. She lived with me as she went through chemo and the accompanying treatments, so I know how cancer takes a toll on a body and the widespread pain it causes. I also know how hard it is when you want to help the one you love but feel powerless to really make a difference.

I am also sorry about the "life stuff" you have had to deal with. None of it is easy or fair. I understand a small part about the drug abuse you described. I have had close family and friends who struggled with addiction. Again, I know how hard it is when you want to help but can't. We can be there to support these loved ones. We can hope. We can pray. But in the final analysis, it is their battle, not ours.

Because you are so young, I think there is an additional element of the "it's not fair" factor. No child should have to deal with the things you have had to face. I'm so sorry. I hope this perspective will help.

Gold is not valuable when it is sitting passively and safely in the ground; it makes its mark when it is refined by fire! Welcome to the fire. The bad news is also your good news. Stuff happens to all of us. It is not the content of the problems but how we respond to them that builds a strong foundation for our future. It's the way we face up to these difficult situations that forms the basic building blocks of our character—the very definition of our inner heart and soul.

In your letter, you talked about being a leader. Throughout history, many great people have learned how to overcome defeat with determination and optimism. They viewed their failures and setbacks as opportunities for growth and improvement. Use your resources and your grit to fight back, to figure out creative ways to address your problems, and to make your dream work!

How did the Wright Brothers teach us to fly? How did Henry Ford show us how to drive? How did the Beatles invite us to sing along in perfect harmony? They taught us these things after they had learned how to do them right, with experience, elbow grease, and persistence. The great ones—the ones we remember and talk about—failed hundreds of times before we ever even heard of them. But they didn't give up.

Here are my suggestions that might help you get through a tough day.

- *Don't panic. Stay calm. When darkness begins to envelope me and I am facing a problem, I remind myself to slow down, think positive thoughts, and take slow, deep breaths.*

- *Analyze the roots of the problem. Ask yourself questions like, "What is really happening here?" and "Who is to blame for this?" If it is you, then change your attitude or your approach. If it is someone else, then let him or her deal with it. Refuse to let someone else's issues ruin your life. Define the actual content of the problem, and make sure you understand what is really going on.*

- *Ask yourself, "What can I learn from this? How will this make me a better person?" Most of our problems are what I call learning blessings. It's so hard to understand these life lessons when we are surrounded by challenges, but let the blessings teach you. Learn from the moments.*

- *You will not always find the solution on your first try. Sometimes, you will follow the best action plan and you will win. Sometimes, you will lose. That is life. Thomas Edison understood this when he said, "I have not failed. I've just found 10,000 ways that won't work." He was not only great at inventing things, he was pretty good at inventing truths, too.*

I believe that someday you will look back on your life and see that the reason you became a great man was because you never let your life be mediocre. You will make it to the top of the mountain, and you will learn how to successfully navigate the falls before, during, and after your quest. Success does not mean you never fail; it just means you have figured out how to fall and how to make it work for you.

I am glad you shared your thoughts about being yourself. It seems you have the same problem I still deal with—wanting everyone to like me. But it's unattainable. Not everyone will like you. I had a counselor tell me one time that not everyone liked Jesus, the most famous and respected individual in history, so why did I think everyone would like me? That was a huge eye opener, and it made perfect sense. There is absolutely no way that everyone will like me all the time. It will never happen. NEVER.

So I have to act like me. That doesn't mean I have to act the same way all the time. There are many pieces that compose our personalities. We all behave a little differently depending on who we are with. That is not a weakness or a fault; it is respect for others so you can relate to them and understand them better.

On the other hand, living a constant lie—when we are not being true to ourselves—is a detriment to our own emotional health. And it's not fair to the friends and family who aren't allowed to see us for who we really are. It's important to be sensitive to others. It's not okay to be a phony.

You can be versatile, communicate effectively with many different personality types, and still be true to yourself. An example of this can be seen in Maggie, the character played by Julia Roberts in **The Runaway Bride***. Maggie had no idea how she liked her eggs, but she fooled herself into thinking that she liked them the same way as whatever guy she was with.*

Maggie was the ultimate people pleaser. Imagine how liberating it was when she finally discovered her preference for Eggs Benedict.

Usually, we pretend to be someone we are not because we don't want to cause conflict. Life can seem so much easier when we are liked. But in reality, we are being unfair to our true sense of self. We will never discover who we are or what we passionately believe if we are afraid to show others our authenticity.

You mentioned the pressure that comes from being a leader, and I agree that leaders are often expected to present a positive front, no matter what. I think some of the worst advice we have been conditioned to accept is that leaders have to keep smiling, even when things are falling apart. Sometimes, the best thing a leader can do is to step back, take a break, and tell the team what is going on. I think this approach has multiple benefits. The truth is out in the open, the team knows what's up, and the leader can receive some much-needed help.

This is called transparency, and it is healthy, honest, and genuine. Being vulnerable is something that is very hard to do, especially for males. Being vulnerable opens up the risk of getting hurt. But if you are secure with who you are, you can use your weaknesses to become stronger. And that's a good thing.

While I don't believe we should pretend that our lives are always filled with sunshine and flowers, there are boundaries to keep in mind. When things are blue, you don't have to be like Eeyore, always walking around with a cloud over your head and waiting for the next drops of rain to fall. Sometimes a situation calls for you to keep smiling, at least for a while. If I am giving a motivational presentation on an Eeyore-ish kind of day, I make a wise decision to suck it up and stay strong so that I can inspire others. But later—when it's appropriate—I quietly share my burden with a friend. This way, I can hold off the rain and bring sunshine to those who need it more than I do that morning. But I am still acknowledging that I am going to need some help and support later in the afternoon. This is a very powerful approach to dealing with others while you are facing your own challenges, and it is truly genuine because you are in charge of what you do.

There are also times when I need to heal and I just need some personal time to myself. In that case, my needs come first. I have to take care of myself before I can effectively help someone else. This isn't mean. It's being honest. It's self-preservation.

I want to thank you for your very sweet words about my program. I really do appreciate them. Sometimes my job can be difficult. I go in and do a program, and afterwards, I'm not really sure what part of my message made an impact. Thanks for telling me what affected you.

I think the best advice I can give you is to stop concentrating on who you are not. Start developing who are. That is how you build your dream. Keep your head up. Be kind, but remember to take care of you. You are not going to be great someday.   You already are great. Believe it.

All the best,
Harriet Turk

Harriet's Heart

Some people will like you when you are fake, and some people won't. Some people will like you when you are real, and some people won't. So you might as well be real.

Reflections

- Why are we afraid to be ourselves? Is it easier for you to try to meet the expectations of others than to be true to yourself? Why or why not?

- Have you put on your "happy pants" or "happy face" even when you don't feel happy on the inside? How did that make you feel?

- When you *are* having a bad day and it's not the right time to let others know that you are feeling down, how do you cope with your feelings?

CHAPTER FIVE

WHEN NO ONE FOLLOWS THE LEADER

"I work so hard for my school. I try to plan great activities and dances but not many people come. I get so tired of trying and not getting better results. What should I do?" said Kelsey.

Kelsey was the president of the student council, and her comments and demeanor surprised me. We'd just had a great assembly in the school auditorium. There had been over 2,000 students in attendance. Their enthusiasm had given me the impression that they loved their school. What did I miss?

"Your student body seemed pretty excited to me, Kelsey. It looks like you and the leadership team are doing your job. What have you tried that hasn't worked?" I asked.

She sighed with frustration and launched into a litany of negatives. "I've tried everything. We haven't had much participation in dances in a long time, and I really thought that I could change things. I worked hard to make them more fun. The student council sponsored more fundraisers than ever before, and we hired a band for homecoming instead of a DJ. We thought that would help. It didn't. We've increased the amount of activities after sporting events, and we've tried lunchtime events. Our pep rallies are okay, but it's always the same people who are involved. It's just depressing. I feel like a failure."

I could tell that Kelsey had her heart in the right place, and she really did want her campus to be successful. But there were definitely some issues that needed to be addressed. It was evident that she felt *personally* responsible for the failure of the entire student council program and that was an unrealistic assessment. This was a team problem, not an individual one. One person can't bring down an entire program, and one person isn't responsible for supporting school spirit throughout an entire student body. Kelsey needed a break. She was overstressed and it was affecting her judgment.

I had some time before I had to leave the school, so I asked her if she had time to talk with me. Luckily, the leadership class was scheduled for the next period, so I could meet with Kelsey and the entire class.

The activities adviser was happy for the opportunity to brainstorm with me because he was feeling as dejected as his student council president. "We've worked really hard to create fun campaigns for our school, but the student body just doesn't care. It's February and the student council term for these kids is almost over. They think this campus is hopeless and their efforts were in vain," he said.

It was time for me to roll up my sleeves. We had some serious work to do. I started by asking a key question, "How many of you love to dress up or wear costumes for spirit days?" All but three hands shot up. I zeroed in on the three who didn't like to participate. "I'm on your team," I said to the naysayers. "I used to hate to dress up, too. School color day was okay. Jersey day, maybe. But every year that I was on student council the group planned costume days and rarely did any of them appeal to me."

I turned my attention back to the entire class and asked them to list some of their favorite dress-related days. The answers ranged from pirate day to superhero day to tacky tourist day. "And what percentage of your students dressed up on those days?" I asked.

Their faces fell as they reported that only about 20 percent of students participated on a regular basis. The negative comments began spouting out. "We don't understand why so few participate." "It could have been so fun!" "Our school is so lame."

I smiled at them. We had just identified the first problem that needed to be solved. These leaders loved their themed concepts, but they were alone in their enthusiasm. The large majority of their followers on campus did not share in their conceptual creativity. Kelsey and her leadership peers didn't do it intentionally. They wanted everyone to participate. But the students they were serving weren't interested in the activities that were being selected.

I explained the problem and the solution to the class. "Don't blame the lack of excitement on the other students. Instead, take the time to really evaluate the likes and dislikes of the student body. Come up with activities they will enjoy instead of focusing on your own wants and needs. When leaders plan for themselves rather than the people they are serving, the number of people participating will always be small."

One major problem had been identified and it was time to continue our discussion. "Give me three reasons why students aren't coming to the dances and other activities."

"No one cares. That's the problem," said one of the leaders.

"Can you be more specific?" I asked. Blank stares.

I have been involved with student activities most of my life, and I speak to schools and organizations about the importance of student leadership. I have to admit that when I look back on my own student council experiences in high school, I don't remember ever looking to see if someone outside my group of friends was involved in council-sponsored events. I just made sure that my friends were there.

It seemed like it was the same with this group. They were using the attendance of a few friends to gauge the interests of many. They could not understand why more students were not at their events, so they assumed that no one cared. I disagree.

I think one of the main reasons that people don't show up for events is because they don't believe it matters. They don't feel like anyone notices. Everyone wants to have a purpose. They want to believe that their presence matters. And if they think that no one notices if they are there or not, then why show up? This is why I believe in the benefits of networking with a variety of clubs and organizations in the school; when you reach out to others, they feel valued and are more invested in the project.

Get the environmental club involved with public relations. Ask the art classes to assist with decorations. Invite service-oriented groups to help select a theme for an event that benefits the school and community. While the leadership class or student council is responsible for leading activities, they don't have to be—and shouldn't be—responsible for selecting and developing all of the activities on their own, without input from others. When one organization or one person tries to do everything for everyone, the plans often fail. A network of people is the best way to go. Connect with others so that everyone feels invested. Give people a purpose and let them know that their help and their attendance is valued.

And don't forget to ask questions. What are the likes and dislikes of the teens currently on campus? Be the voice for the entire student body. Listen to what they say and involve them in the planning. If everyone is tired of dances but would love a slam poetry hour, then eliminate a dance and add this new activity. If a donkey basketball game has seen better days, plan a dodge ball tournament and watch the number of teams increase. Don't always keep an activity simply because it's always been done. Shake things up!

Kelsey had the best intentions and wanted to change the attitudes of students on campus. She was trying to prove that she was a great leader. Unfortunately, she wasn't involving the students she was supposed to be serving in the decision-making process. She was pursuing specific activities when it was obvious that most students weren't interested, and then assuming that it was the students who were the problem.

What if she had followed these strategies instead?

- *Every leader needs a team.* Every leader needs people who take ownership in a project and invest their time and unique abilities toward accomplishing a shared mission. The best teams include people who have varying viewpoints and aren't afraid to share their ideas. When that happens, you are capturing the true composition of the people you want to serve. Be the leader of the team; don't try to be the entire team.

- *When people believe they own something, they are more likely to work for it.* When students are asked to submit ideas and their ideas are actually heard and discussed, students feel valued. They are more willing to invest their time to make the activity a success, and they are more likely to participate in future events.

- *Many times traditional activities are maintained, not because they work or because people enjoy them, but because "that's what we've always done."* Sometimes traditions need to be put to rest. When something has run its course, let it go. Generate excitement for new opportunities.

- *On the other hand, if a campaign or activity is working, don't change it simply because you want to try something new.* Keep the momentum going and continue to make improvements. But be careful about removing components that people love. You won't know unless you ask, so ask people what they most enjoy about the event. Why do they keep coming back?

It's not the campaign that decides whether or not a leader is great, it's the execution of the campaign. And when the student body actively participates because they want to and not because they have to, that's the mark of great leadership. When I left that day, Kelsey and her team were buzzing with ideas. They were brainstorming about ways to get more students involved and talking about how they could encourage and empower their classmates to play an active role in the decision making. As I walked out the door, I overheard a student say, "Guys, let's figure out a way to go to them instead of expecting them to come to us."

That's leadership!

Harriet's Heart

Leadership is not just about shining your own light; it's about helping others to shine their lights, too.

Reflections

- Is there a cause you are passionate about? Do your friends or family members share your passion?

- What does it mean to have the group "buy into" the project? Does it make the leader's job easier when they do?

- If you are in charge of a group and no one is following your directions, what steps should you take to remedy this problem?

CHAPTER SIX

NO MAJOR. NO PROBLEM.

"You're a senior? That's awesome. Where are you going to school next year?" I asked.

I thought it was a safe question. It was the same one I had been asked 5,434 times during my senior year of high school. I thought it was the right question, but from the look on Sam's face, I could tell that it wasn't a question he wanted to answer.

"I have no idea. I don't even know if I'll go to college," said Sam. "My parents tell me there is no reason to go because I have no idea what I want to do in the future. I don't know what to major in. I'm interested in a lot of things. I'd like to go to college, but I don't know what I want to study."

I had to laugh. It wasn't the empathetic response Sam had been expecting.

"Why is that funny?" He narrowed his eyes.

"I'm sorry. I guess it's because I went through five majors and three advisers during my freshman year. I had absolutely no idea what I wanted to major in. Every month it was something different. My ever-evolving choice of majors became a big joke among my friends," I said.

Sam was not amused. "I have a high score on the ACT and scholarships to two different schools, but my parents say that it's ridiculous to go if I don't have a plan. They keep pushing me to be a doctor, but I know I don't want to do that. I'm just so confused."

I could sympathize with Sam. At that moment, I wanted to grab his cell phone and call his parents. Did they have their lives mapped out when they were 18? Why do parents put such pressure on their children?

I was 17 when I graduated from high school. I went to a college prep high school that had prepared me well for college. I had good grades and was active in school. But I had also scored a 15 on my ACT, including a 10 in math. With these scores, I had to enter college on probation and take courses in remedial math. I'm not proud of that, but math was never my strong point. I am motivational, not mathematical. And what I had told Sam was true. I changed my major five times during my first year of college. Was it a big deal? On paper, yes. But in how it affected my life in the long run, no.

Would I advise anyone else to change their major five times in their freshman year? Probably not. But I would advise them to take their time and think everything through before declaring a major. Get your required courses out of the way first, and while you are doing that, evaluate each subject and determine if any of them spark a special interest. Take diverse electives and use them as opportunities to discover new strengths and interests. In time, you will narrow down what you want to do. Trust me. You will figure it out.

Today, I have a Master of Science in Criminal Justice, and even though I am not following this career path right now, my professional life is just fine. Over the years, I have pursued many different careers. I have worked in the criminal justice field, served as a coordinator for youth programs, and been a consultant for the National Safety Council and Students Against Destructive Decisions (SADD). I have also worked as a flight attendant, a pharmaceutical sales representative, an adjunct professor at a university, and a professional speaker. A few times, I did several of those jobs at the same time.

I understand that parents want their children to have a plan. I also understand that children want to please their parents. Sometimes, this can be a match made in heaven, but sometimes, it is a recipe for disaster. When parents are constantly monitoring their child's grades, activities, and social interactions, the pressure to perform can be too intense. Instead of serving as a motivator, overzealous parental guidance can destroy a child's aspirations. The future can seem like an obstacle instead of an opportunity. At this point, depending on the teen's personality, he or she will try harder, resulting in even more pressure, or he or she will give up entirely.

I can't tell you how many times a student has said to me, "I really want to major in this when I go to college, but my parents say I can make more money if I major in that. They say they won't pay for college if I don't go to the school of their choice and if I don't choose the career that they think is best for me."

While the parents usually have good intentions, the

41

pressure from this constrictive approach is too much. A teen in this situation feels like he or she has no control over his or her own life. In Sam's case, the desire to do well and make good choices became less about him and more about his parents. He felt pressured to serve his parents' goals, so he put aside his own ideas for his future. His parents thought they knew what was best for Sam, not realizing that the best way for anyone to accomplish a goal is to own it.

Sometimes, I hear students say, "My parents don't understand me. They just want me to be like them." In reality, this may or may not be true. But I have discovered that even if the teen only thinks that this is what the parents want, then the discussion is over. Period.

Other times, parents want to help but feel isolated. They may not have experience with educational planning, or they may not be getting any cooperation from their teenager. In this case, it's the teen's turn to take more responsibility in getting parents involved in the process.

Don't be afraid to get your parents involved! Talk to them about your goals or what you might be interested in studying. Let them know what's going on in your heart and in your mind. If they don't have the answers, they might have a friend or an experienced contact that can help answer your questions. If your parents aren't open to helping you flush out some ideas, ask another family member, a guidance counselor, or a trusted adult.

When I was in high school, I thought I wanted to be a speech pathologist. I shared this goal with a friend's mother since she had worked in the field. She was able to take me to a school where other speech pathologists were using their skills to help hearing-impaired children develop language skills. Even though I didn't end up in that career, I still remember that afternoon and everything I learned on that day. The experience was invaluable, and it wouldn't have happened had I not reached out to an experienced adult.

Never be afraid to share your dreams and goals with people. It doesn't mean you are making a commitment. Instead, you are making a wise choice to explore something that interests you.

Should you go to college? Yes, if you really want to.

Do you need to know right now, at this very moment, what you want to do with the rest of your life before you decide what school to attend? No, you do not.

Should you visit a few college campuses and find one where you feel comfortable? Absolutely. You may think you want to attend a huge Division I school, and maybe that is the right choice for you. But a smaller, community college may end up being a better fit. Or maybe a technical or trade school is more suited to your needs.

Remember. You are creating a plan for *your* life.

It's a balancing act. You do need to seek guidance from trusted adults. Don't try to figure it out all by yourself. At the same time, don't lose sight of what you want to do by trying to please everyone but you.

Be patient with yourself. Take one step at a time. You'll get there. If I can do it, so can you!

Harriet's Heart

Knowledge isn't power until you put it into action.

Reflections

- If nothing were standing in your way, what would your plans be for the first five years after high school?

- If you asked your parents/guardians what they would do differently if they could go back in time and plan for life after high school graduation, what do you think their answers would be?

- Ask them. Were you surprised by their answers? Do their answers match any of your ideas about your own future plans?

CHAPTER SEVEN

DIVORCE HURTS

"I've been so depressed lately. My parents are getting a divorce. I don't want them to separate. I'm so mad at my mom because she kicked my dad out. It has ruined our family. I hate my life now," said Kendall. "What should I do?"

Kendall had waited until the last person left. She was smiling, so I thought she was going to say something upbeat, lighthearted, and happy. I was wrong. Her words jolted me.

Ugh. I gave Kendall a frozen smile, stalled, and tried to think of a response. Meanwhile, I was also thinking, "Great. My son is probably asking someone else this very same question about his own parents. This is too close for comfort. I've been that parent who kicked someone out and asked for a divorce."

No one wins in this situation: not the parent or the child or the motivational speaker. Divorce hurts.

Everyone thinks that motivational speakers with the

confidence to take the stage have it all together and that our lives are perfect. That would not be me. My life would make a really great reality show and not the kind I would want people to watch.

I took a deep breath and began to give this sweet girl some hope with words that might make my heart feel better, too. "I won't lie to you. Divorce is horrible. I am so sorry you have to deal with it. Most little girls dream of the day they will get married. I've never heard of a little girl who dreamed of the day she would get divorced."

I continued, "I'm sure your mom is incredibly depressed, too. Kicking your dad out didn't happen overnight. And even though you think you know about everything that has happened in your house, in reality, you don't. So how many people in your family are divorcing?"

She held up two fingers.

I smiled and said, "Yep. It takes both sides to marry and an equal number to divorce. There is a ton of emotion flying around all of you. Everyone is hurting. Everyone is angry. Everyone is confused, and everyone is clueless!"

Kendall nodded vigorously.

"During this difficult time, you can't blame your mom. She is your mom. You can't blame your dad. He's your dad. You will probably be put in some unfair situations and you may be asked to take sides, but DON'T DO IT," I said firmly.

"Why not?" asked Kendall.

"Well, do you love both of them?"

"Yes," she replied.

"Always remember that, okay? You may be in for

some tough times, whether it's being shuffled between new living accommodations, making changes at home, or not having your parents show up on time like they always did before. But I want to encourage you to keep your head up. Sometimes, one day at a time is too long. One hour at a time may be all you can handle. Make it through one hour. Keep going. One hour at a time."

"How do I do that?" asked Kendall.

"Just keep remembering that they are hurting, too."

"But why couldn't she give my dad another chance?" she asked.

I replied, "I have no way of knowing for sure, but maybe your mom had already given him several chances. Maybe in her mind, he was out of chances. But whether your parents stay married or not, you have no control over it. Remembering that you can't control their marriage is a key step in managing your life right now. Over the years, I have learned some other things you can do to feel in control of your own life."

Surviving Divorce 101: Let Me Count the Ways.

- *Remember that the divorce is not your fault.* Relationships, especially marriages, are complex. The only people who truly know what is happening in the marriage are the ones who are married. You are not to blame for this breakup. You will be affected, but it is not your fault. No matter what you may hear, no matter what you may feel, and no matter what you may want to think, you must believe and remember that the divorce of your parents is not your fault.

- *Remember that you are loved.* You may have heard your parents say cruel things to each other, including "I hate you." This is their anger talking. These phrases do not apply to you. You are their child and they love you very much. Their marriage is broken, not their relationship with you.

- *Find ways to release your anger, your sadness, or any other hurtful feelings.* Divorce hurts everyone involved. If you don't feel like you can talk to your parents, write down your feelings. Find ways to recharge your soul. This may be through exercise or a hobby or even hanging out with friends. Find healthy ways to escape. Concentrate on being healthy even when it may be easier to act like a sloth. Be active. Go outside and get some fresh air. Take a walk. Go for a run.

- *Understand that sometimes you will feel bad and that it's okay to feel this way.* You are in a situation that will create sadness and anger. That's what family breakups do. For some reason, society teaches us that we should keep a stiff upper lip, even when we are sad. But our lives are not always going to be happy. It's okay to feel depressed.

- *Remember that one day your new normal will be okay.* You will adjust. Hang on. It may not be perfect and you may wish for the times when your parents were married, but the new normal will be okay. In the meantime, it's okay to take care of yourself. Don't worry about fixing your parents.

As we talked, Kendall seemed relieved that she was not alone in her distress about divorce. While my words were intended to comfort her, I found that my attitude was improving, too. So what can any of us do when faced with chaos?

Hang on. Whether it's a divorce or another type of situation that brings sadness and upheaval to your world, tell yourself, "I will get through this!" True character is not defined by how we respond in the happy times. Those times are easy. True character is determined by the way we fight to survive during the difficult times.

"Divorce is a roller coaster," I told Kendall. "Fasten your seat belt and hang on tight. You will go up and down and all around. But just like any other wild ride, this particular journey will come to an end and you will walk away better equipped for the other twists and turns that life brings. And trust me, there will be other roller coasters along the way."

Kendall smiled and simply said, "Thanks!"

That afternoon, I went home and hugged my own son a little tighter than usual. I reminded him for the zillionth time how much I loved him and how happy I am to be his mom.

Harriet's Heart

Life is great. Life is tough. But it's

never perfect and

it's never predictable. Roll with it and

keep going.

Just keep GOING!

Reflections

- Have you or someone close to you been a child of divorce?

- How has this affected his/her/your life in positive and negative ways?

- What strategies have helped you cope with a parental divorce or other major stressors in your life?

CHAPTER EIGHT

YOU ARE BEAUTIFUL

"Ms. Turk, how did you stop being bulimic?"

Before I could answer, another young woman joined in. "Like, how did you stop thinking you were fat? How did you get to the place where you could eat without wanting to throw up afterward?"

I opened my mouth to respond, only to be met with a question from yet another girl. "Are you okay now, or is it still difficult for you?"

I started laughing and held up my hand. "Hold on. I know what you are really asking."

It was likely that these girls were curious about my story because it was their story, too. They might not have been suffering from an eating disorder, but most girls have issues with their body image. These three young women wanted to know how to feel better about themselves and the way they looked.

It never ceases to amaze me that a three-minute story about my struggles with bulimia during adolescence can create such a stir. I get more emails, Facebook messages, letters, and phone calls about this subject than any other topic I speak about.

Almost always, these messages include comments from young people expressing dismay over their own physical appearances. "I'm so fat. I hate the way I look." "If I just looked thinner, then my life would be happy." "You probably don't understand, but I feel disgusting."

My response is always the same. "I do understand, more than you know."

I can't remember a time in my high school or college years when I liked the way I looked. There were times when I hated myself less, but I can't remember ever being happy with my appearance. It didn't matter that I was part of the popular crowd on campus. It didn't matter that I won awards or was a class officer. All that mattered was being skinny. I thought that if I was skinny, I would be beautiful. And if I were beautiful, I would be somebody.

I am amazed when I see pictures of myself from high school. I looked fine, but I didn't see it that way. I had punished my body in horrible ways to maintain that appearance. Was it worth it? No.

With the amount of laxatives I consumed, it's a wonder I could ever go out in public. I wasn't very good at making myself throw up until I learned a horrible trick. It was the same trick that helped to kill a famous star from the 1970s. When I heard how she used it to fuel her eating disorder, I wasn't horrified. Instead, I immediately added this activity to my own bulimic routine. It was crazy behavior that I justified in my quest for perfection.

When I pause today and reflect on my obsessive desire to be thin, I often wonder what my criteria was for being skinny enough. I knew I wanted to be thin but there was no finish line I could cross that would have let me know when my goal had been achieved.

If you really think about it, it's no wonder that so many women struggle with eating disorders. Since the beginning of time, women have been valued for their beauty—from Cleopatra to Marilyn Monroe, from Britney Spears to Beyoncé. Men are more likely to be remembered for strong personality traits like intelligence, power, or confidence. But when a woman displays these qualities, it is still her physical appearance that is the center of attention.

We are conditioned to believe that thin is sexy. Give a babe a bikini and her perceived value increases, as long as she holds on to her looks. You don't believe me? Look at any fashion or beauty magazine. Take the time to study the majority of women featured in today's blockbuster films and popular television shows. Over time, we start to believe the pervasive messages of the media, and we mimic what we are told is beautiful. We begin to focus so much on *who we are not* that we forget to develop *who we can be*. We recognize our perceived flaws, but we ignore our best qualities. That's not beauty; that's bogus.

I'll never forget watching Jenny McCarthy's appearance on Rosie O'Donnell's talk show. In the 1990s, Jenny was a popular model, actress, and the host of a show on MTV. During the interview, she disclosed that she wanted to tell girls the real deal about her body. She pulled out a poster of herself and a Sharpie pen, and she begin noting all of the imperfections that had been deleted from the poster's final version, including a huge fever blister that appeared on the day of the photo shoot and a large birthmark on one of her legs. As she continued to physically draw in her imperfections, I was happy, but I was also sad. Because the beautiful Jenny McCarthy has imperfections on her body, just like you and I do. But we weren't allowed to see them. Why? Because Hollywood is intent on making celebrities look perfect. Unless you are a comedian or a character actor where beauty and looks can be a physical liability, the entertainment industry—and the media that covers it— are relentless in their depiction of perfection.

Without professional makeup, perfected camera angles, contouring, and Photoshop, most celebrities would look. . .normal! Many of the sexy stars in our social universe look completely different without makeup. You wouldn't even recognize them. But they have to maintain an idealized image in order to sell their movies, magazines, and products. The average woman can't compete with that, and we shouldn't have to. Let Hollywood be Hollywood. Let you be you. I would respect and admire a genuine person any day over a synthesized celebrity.

It's normal to have certain ideas about how we want to look. When I was younger, I wished I could look like my two best friends. It's interesting that when I reflect on the way these sweet girls actually looked, they were very different in appearance. One was tall and blond and the other was petite with long, dark hair. I now realize that I admired them because of the kind of special friends they were. Yes, I liked the way they looked, but I loved who they were. And while I was spending my time wanting to be like other girls, I later discovered that there were people out there who wanted to be like ME! You might be surprised to know that while you are wishing you were like someone else, someone else might be wishing that they were more like you. It's true.

So what would happen if all of us—girls *and* boys—rejected an unattainable image of perfection and started focusing on making the most of who we are? What if we concentrated on being healthy versus being perfect?

For many young people with an eating disorder, the first step in being healthy is realizing that food is not the enemy. The healthiest diet is to eat often and in small packages. NEVER skip breakfast or you may find yourself sleeping through your first hour class. Eat something for breakfast: half of a sandwich, a cup of yogurt, a banana, a bowl of cereal...something. Keep doing that throughout the day and you will have an energetic, healthy, and awake body. Just like a car needs gas to run, you need food to fuel your body.

It took years for me to believe this, but I finally learned to eat like a normal human is supposed to eat. I understand that I can't eat an entire chocolate cake and expect to stay in shape. But I also know that no matter how much broccoli I eat, I can't expect to have a body like Selena Gomez.

Another step on the road to recovery is to make a conscious effort to embrace your differences. Even as an adult, I can get caught in a trap of thinking I am less than someone else. One of my favorite examples of this happened when my son and I were visiting my younger sister. When we got in the car to go home, my son enthusiastically said, "Mom, you and Aunt Mary look just alike except she is so much skinnier than you."

I faked a smile but I was horrified. I thought, "My son thinks I'm fat!" When I calmed down, I realized that what my five-year-old had said was true. My sister was skinnier than me. She's always been tiny. That's her body shape. But my son's comment wasn't meant as a criticism. It was simply an observation that we are not the same. My sister has some great physical qualities but so do I. This is not about appearance; it's about being unique.

Do I absolutely love every one of my body parts and think I could be on the cover of a magazine? No. Do I care about being as externally beautiful as much as I once did? Sometimes. But I have learned to accept the beauty that comes from being myself.

We all possess beauty and value. It's the genuine essence of who we are as unique individuals that guarantees it. We need to focus on our inside as much as we do on our outside. When our image overshadows our integrity, that is a problem. As the years go by, it will be your integrity and character that determine your true beauty. Believe it.

Realize that no one is perfect and that you are valuable.

You are beautiful. Always.

Harriet's Heart

We all want to change something
about ourselves. Sometimes, you can.
Sometimes, you can't.
Learn to accept and work with what
you have.

Reflections

- Why do we concentrate so much on our outward appearance?

- Do you have a distorted image of yourself? If so, how does this impact your everyday life? If not, do you know someone who does, and what are the effects of this false image on his or her life?

- What can we do to concentrate more on our integrity than on our physical image?

CHAPTER NINE

THE FUNNY GUY

"I think you have a really cool job, and I wondered if it would be okay if I emailed you sometime," said Jackson.

He was a high school student who had just attended one of my presentations. It was obvious he had enjoyed the talk and was interested in my line of work. Maybe I was talking to a future motivational speaker. There are a lot of uninspired young people out there. The world needed this spark of encouragement standing before me.

"Sure," I said. "I even have a little resource manual for people who want to become speakers that may give you some direction." But just when I thought I had him sized up, he threw me a curve.

"Oh, I don't want to be a speaker. I just think you'd be cool to talk to," he said. "I don't have anyone to talk to. I think you have a cool job, and you seem really nice. I just thought I could email you sometime."

"Sure," I replied as I handed him my business card. "But why don't you have anyone to talk to?"

His answer was incisive. "I have lots of friends, but no one really cares when the tough stuff starts. I am a really funny guy. But when I'm not funny, people don't listen. They don't take me seriously, so I don't feel like I have anyone who really listens when I need to talk. Since you don't know me, I was hoping that you would listen and maybe help me sometimes."

A class clown with a deep soul. That may sound like an oxymoron but it is common among funny people. Most comedians have a deep, dark side. They grew up with pain and used their humor to survive the demons of despair and depression. The list is long and loaded with familiar names: Louie Anderson, Jim Carrey, George Lopez, Ellen DeGeneres, Roseanne Barr, and many others. Laughing on the outside; crying on the inside.

I wondered if this was what it was like to be a circus clown. The focus is on the painted smile and a strategically-timed squirt of seltzer water. But what happens when a clown needs someone to take him seriously?

As Jackson walked away, I realized that here was another student who barely knew me but wanted to be a part of my life. This young man felt safe confiding in me but not in anyone who was a real friend. Why?

In this case, Jackson didn't think that he had any real friends who accepted and loved him unconditionally. Instead of allowing Jackson to be real, they only seemed to be attentive when he was funny. It was a dilemma. Be the life of the party and everyone gathers around, but begin sharing your fears and failures, and the room empties faster than someone can unfriend you on Facebook.

Coincidentally, the guidance counselor approached as Jackson was walking away so I asked her about him. She broke out into a huge grin and said, "That guy is one of the most popular seniors in school. He is hysterical. Everyone loves him!" My heart ached for Jackson. He must have felt like he was always on stage.

Remember Robin Williams? He was a brilliant actor and comedian who died tragically when he committed suicide in 2014. This popular, comedic actor didn't die surrounded by his friends and family. He chose to die alone. Even though he brought joy to the world through his jokes, comedy routines, and movies, he constantly struggled with drug addiction and severe depression. We only saw the public side of Robin Williams, and most of us enjoyed what we saw. But deep down, Robin Williams had very human battles. His story reminds us that even funny people have issues, and they need to be loved and supported for who they are both on and off the stage.

A few minutes before, I had been shyly approached by one of the school's most popular students. It seemed to me that he was searching for acceptance, not just when he was funny, but also at times when he was not feeling so comical. As I considered Jackson's situation, I smiled to myself because how many times in my life have I done the very same thing that Jackson was doing now? I may not be known as the funny one, but I rarely let people into my world. The nature of a motivational speaker's job often requires me to give the impression that I am a superhero of inspiration. Because of that, I am reluctant to be transparent and vulnerable.

Friends I haven't seen in a while ask how I'm doing. No matter how things are going, my answer is always a predictable and guarded, "I'm fine." It's the same when family members ask. My wall goes up. "I'm fine. Really good. Just been busy."

Busy doing what? Keeping people out. I don't want to bother people with my issues. Or maybe I don't think they will really care. Because sometimes, when I have shared a problem or two, I have heard, "You are smart. You are a survivor. You will figure it out. After all, you are a motivational speaker." And those words weren't validating at a time when I just wanted someone to listen and understand.

I'm not Edison or Einstein. I'm not even Tina Fey. I am just Harriet. I have good qualities. I am loyal. I am a good listener. I never let failure define my life. But if you believe for one moment that I am cruising through life without any problems just because I am a motivational speaker, then you would be wrong.

Life can be difficult, and it requires each of us to be resilient, optimistic, stubborn, decisive, wise, and committed to an emotionally healthy mindset. It requires us to seek healthy, supportive friendships. So when my family and friends told me that I would figure it out on my own, here is what I really wanted to say, "Please listen to me. I just told you about something that is really bothering me. It was hard for me to open up and share that with you. Because I was willing to take that leap, I really need you to listen and be supportive. You may not be able to solve my problems, and in fact, I may not need you to. But right now, I just need someone to be my friend. Right now, I need someone to listen."

That is what I want Jackson to say the next time he

is feeling down. I want him to have the courage to seek support, and I want his friends to step up and show him that they will be there for him, even when he doesn't feel like being the funny guy. And that is what I hope you will say when you need some extra encouragement.

Imagine what would happen if we allowed people into our lives. What if—instead of hiding who we are and playing a certain role—we could just be ourselves and people would still be there for us? How much better and more authentic would our lives be?

I never heard from Jackson, and I wonder if he ever found someone to talk to. I hope he doesn't feel like he's alone. Because being surrounded by people but feeling like you are all alone is one of the loneliest places to be. Believe me, I know.

And it's not funny.

Harriet's Heart

When I return to me, I am free.

Reflections

- Is it easier for you to wear a mask than to be your true, genuine self?

- When you reach out to your friends for help, are they willing and able to listen to you? If not, what are some things you can do to improve these communications? Are there trusted adults who would be willing to listen?

- Why do you think the ones who *are* so funny often seem to hide the most pain?

CHAPTER TEN

YOU DON'T NEED A SOMEBODY

"Can you help me figure out what's wrong with me?"
"How do I get a boyfriend?"
"Why don't girls like me?"
"Girls only like the mean guys. I'm too nice. I guess that's why I can't get a girlfriend."
"If I acted like a slut, guys would like me. Because I won't, I can't get a boyfriend."
"I just want someone to love me."

We all want to know we are special, and it can be fun to be in a relationship. But it's not okay to use our relationship status to define our self-worth. When I present workshops to teens, I sometimes use a question box that allows attendees to ask any question by dropping an anonymous note into the box. Without exception, the number one question is, "How do I get a boyfriend/girlfriend?"

My advice is always the same. You do not "get" someone. Just be yourself. Make him or her search for you. The right person will find you.

In response, the young people all cheer. But while they are cheering for the moment, I know that the majority of them won't apply this advice in real life. Most teens, especially girls, feel empowered when they are with a group. When they are separated and alone, many of them believe that they must be in a relationship to be considered good enough. This is also one of the main reasons why I believe girls and guys stay in relationships longer than they should. The stigma of being alone is worse than the reality of maintaining an unhealthy relationship.

We all want a happily ever after, but simply being in a relationship doesn't ensure that the stars will line up and your future will be defined by fairy tale bliss. Real relationships are tough, especially in adolescence when kids are maturing and learning how to successfully deal with a variety of complex issues. That's why, for many teens, it makes sense to be free and have fun with friends during this turbulent time of life. You will have plenty of time for a serious commitment and the hard work that comes with it later in life. For now, enjoy the fun part of being a teenager.

Unfortunately, societal norms—often displayed through songs, movies, or the expectations of our friends—tell us that we need a special someone to make us happy and to prove our worth to the world. Because of this, we might feel pressured to be part of a couple. We might settle for someone who isn't right for us, maybe even someone who mistreats us. Or we might reach out to someone we like and get rejected. We begin to believe the lie that no one wants us and that we will always be alone.

When I was in high school, I went out with a guy from a rival school. He was so good looking that I couldn't even believe he was interested in me. Physically, he was exactly my type—athletic, tall, blue eyes, blond hair. Years later, I can still see his face. He really liked me and most of my friends were jealous that I was the one he wanted.

For a few dates, things seemed great. We went to parties, and because he was popular, I got noticed, too. He took me to expensive restaurants. He drove a sports car. As we say in the South, "He was all that and a bag of chips." I couldn't believe how lucky I was. But after the fourth date, I realized that I could not waste one more night on this guy.

Why? On the surface, he was amazing. But we had nothing in common. We didn't share similar interests, and his intellect left me craving a stimulating conversation. It got to the point that, when he began speaking, I wanted to firmly press my finger to his lips and say, "Shhhh. Don't talk. Just let me look at you." All of his attributes—his physical appearance, nice car, and popularity—were not enough. He had no depth and no clue as to how to effectively relate to me or the rest of the world. I could have easily been his girlfriend, but why would I want to be? Was it enough to say that I had a good looking boyfriend? Was he enough to make me feel like a valuable person when I was bored out of my mind every time we were together? No and no.

Sadly, just because I got out of that situation doesn't mean I learned from the experience. I went on to stay in other relationships long after learning that the person I was dating wasn't the right one for me. I think a lot of us make this same mistake because we believe that being with someone, even if it's Mr. Wrong, is still better than being alone.

Sometimes, we fool ourselves into believing that the person we are with will change. When I ask people why they stay in an unhealthy relationship, they usually say, "I know he (or she) is really a good person on the inside. I keep hoping he (or she) will start acting like it." Please, repeat after me. *Zebras cannot be monkeys.*

As author and activist Dr. Maya Angelou once said, "When people show you who they are, believe them." Many times, we try to believe in the potential of someone rather than in the reality of who they are. A person may be able to change some of their minor flaws, but it is almost impossible for a person to change the essence of who they are. In other words, stop trying to convince yourself that your zebra is a monkey. You are healthier staying home on a Saturday night than spending time with someone who will never be able to change into a new and improved version of who they are. You cannot control someone else. You can only be in charge of you.

Life is too short to stay with someone who hurts you or someone you fight with too much. Life is too short to be bored or unhappy. Believing in the potential of someone is a noble gesture, but sometimes you have to look at the reality of the situation. If you have given someone multiple chances and you are still unhappy, then it isn't the right relationship for you. A counselor once told me, "When you have done everything you know to do to save a relationship and it hasn't worked, you can walk out the door and close it behind you, knowing you did the best you could."

Having a boyfriend or a girlfriend is supposed to be fun. It's supposed to be something you both want. It's not intended to cause ongoing pain.

So how can you find the person who is right for you?

- *Be yourself.* Every time you try to be someone you are not, it will backfire. It may work for a short amount of time, but it's too hard to maintain. If you want to be an actor, go on Broadway. If you want a real relationship, be yourself.

- *Be confident.* This doesn't mean you walk into a room and steamroller everyone, but be confident that you are just as good and just as valuable as everyone else in that room.

- *Act interested.* If you are interested in someone, act like it. Playing hard to get may not work in your favor. What if he or she doesn't understand that you are playing a game? If you admired someone's performance in the school play or on the basketball court, tell them. If you like what he or she is wearing, say so. Keep it simple, and don't throw yourself at him or her. But don't play games.

- *Take pride in your appearance.* This doesn't mean you have to look perfect. When you look your best, you feel better about yourself. If you are a girl, you don't have to wear a lot of makeup. Most guys don't even like a lot of makeup. And you don't have to dress provocatively for a guy to notice you. Trust me on this one. You are a girl. You get noticed even when you don't try. Guys, take a shower and use soap. Brush your hair. It would be nice to see you in something other than gym shorts and a hoodie.

- *Above all else, present yourself in positive ways that are consistent with the kind of person you are on the inside.* Consider the messages that your personal hygiene and the way you dress are sending to those around you, including the guy or girl who has captured your attention.

Now that you know a few tips about how to approach a boy or a girl, here are some reasons why it's also great to be single.

- *You have the freedom to do what you want.* When you are in a relationship, you are always wondering what the other person is doing or if you should ask him/her to join you in an activity. When you are single, you don't have to do that. You can do whatever you want without feeling guilty for not including your significant other. You can actively pursue a new hobby, get a job, or play a sport without feeling like you have to share your time with someone else. It's okay to be selfish with your time. When you are in a committed relationship and/or married, your decisions are impacted by another person. For now, enjoy your freedom.

- *You can spend as much time with your friends as you*

want. You never have to decide if you will be with your friends on one night of the weekend and your boyfriend/girlfriend on the other night. Your time belongs to you.

- *You don't have to deal with the pressure of spending money to purchase gifts and pay for dates.* It can be fun to buy your boyfriend/girlfriend a special present or splurge on a nice date, but it's hard when your finances are limited. There is also a lot of pressure about what to buy or where to go. When you are single, you don't have to worry about any of this.

- *You never have to hear threats like, "If you loved me, you would (or wouldn't) do this."* That is the most manipulative, selfish line ever invented. When you are single, you don't have to come up with a clever retort for dealing with master manipulations.

- *You have time to find yourself.* You are able to put more energy into developing who you are and who you want to be. You are able spend time creating your own canvas; you can color, scribble, erase, and reinvent who you are. This is time well spent because when you figure out how to be content with yourself, you won't try to use a boyfriend/girlfriend to define your happiness. You will be emotionally satisfied with who you are as a person.

- *You can ditch the drama.* There is always some kind of drama in a relationship—an argument when you least expect it or a "discussion" you don't want to have. One time, when I was conducting a workshop,

I asked for four volunteers: two guys and two girls. After pairing up two couples consisting of a boy and a girl each, we completed the activity. When the workshop was over and students were leaving, I heard a girl screaming at one of the guys who had volunteered. She was accusing him of looking at his female partner too much. The guy was defending himself in every way possible. I had instructed him to look at the girl, but now he paying for it with an unleashing of his girlfriend's insecurity and jealousy. I should have stepped in and helped him out, but she even scared me!

It can be awesome to be in a relationship. It can be equally amazing to be single. In every stage of life, there are seasons. Just because you are not in a relationship now, doesn't mean you'll be single forever. This may not be your time. When the time and the person are right for you, you won't have to force it. You will feel it.

So how can you get a boyfriend/girlfriend? There is no foolproof technique. How can you keep the one you love from leaving? Again, there are no guarantees. Healthy relationships take two people who are willing to do what it takes to make each other happy. Until the time you find the right one, realize that you don't need to be connected to someone to be happy. Be happy today.

Harriet's Heart

One day you will meet the one who

has been looking for you. Until then,

be happy. Have fun.

Live YOUR life.

Reflections

- Do some people stay in a relationship no matter how toxic it is just so they can say they have a girlfriend/boyfriend?

- How can you be happily single when you see so many of your friends in a relationship?

- What are the advantages of not searching for someone and instead concentrating on your own life?

CHAPTER ELEVEN

KEEP BREATHING

Dear Mrs. Turk,

I hope you can help me. You seem like someone I could talk to, and I can't talk to my mom and dad. I think I'm pregnant.

If I am, my mom and dad will kill me. I'm more afraid of them than I am of God. If I am pregnant, I am seriously considering suicide. I don't see a way out of this. My parents will make my life hell. You have no idea how much they will hate me and what I will have to go through.

If I did kill myself, I think God would forgive me. I don't think my parents ever would. Ever. I know they love me, but if I embarrass them, I would never hear the end of it. Please help me. I am so scared, and I don't know what to do.

Sincerely,
Emily

Emily's email was heartbreaking. Sometimes, the messages I received fill me with joy; sometimes, not. This was a not.

I knew how she felt. Emily was more afraid of her parent's reaction to her situation than she was of the situation itself. I could relate to that fear. I grew up in a pretty normal home, but there were times when I lived in complete fear of what my parents would think about some of the choices I made. As a teen, I never thought I was pregnant. But I could imagine how I would have felt if I had been. Who would I have turned to? Probably not my parents.

Emails like this are especially hard for me. I want to help, so I become emotionally invested. I want to know the rest of the story, but most of the time, I don't get to hear it. Because in reality, the young person on the other end of the message is a stranger. I want what's best for all of the kids I speak with, but we really don't know each other. I don't have a direct line into their lives.

I did what I could. I let Emily know that I received her note and that I wanted to be there for her. I tried to offer some advice that might help her navigate this troubling situation.

Dear Emily,

Thank you for reaching out to me. I understand what it's like to be afraid to talk to your parents. When I was your age, I was, too.

Here's your first step. Go buy a pregnancy test. Make sure you are pregnant. I read that tests from the dollar store are just as reliable as tests you find in an expensive drug store, so go buy one. Follow the directions, and then look at the results.

If you are not pregnant, the worry is over. Email me back, and we'll talk about some choices you can make so this won't happen again.

If you are pregnant, I want you to take a deep breath. I want you to realize that this is not the end of the world and that you still have a great life ahead of you. You are a wonderful, beautiful girl, no matter how you feel at this moment. You are a valuable human being, even if you feel like you have royally screwed up. You need to remember that you have worth and things will get better. I believe a baby is always a good thing.

Yes. You will have some serious choices to make. It won't be easy, but you must tell your parents. If you don't feel safe talking to them alone, think of another adult who can talk to your parents with you. I recommend that you tell an adult you trust first, before you go to your parents. He or she can be part of that meeting in your home.

Even though you fear that your parents will hate you, you might be surprised at their reaction. There may be some initial anger which would be totally normal on their part. They are your parents who have invested their love and concern. After their first reaction, their concern will kick in. I believe they will love you unconditionally, even though it may take some time for this to show. But you will never know unless you give them a chance. You are still their child. A parent's love almost always trumps their anger.

If I'm wrong, I promise that I will do whatever I can to find you a safe place and to help you find the resources you need.

All the best,
Harriet Turk

I felt awful for Emily who was faced with the

prospect of a premature pregnancy. But I would feel even worse if she gave up on herself. So here is my challenge to Emily and to anyone who is struggling with a difficult obstacle: I want you to remember that you matter. You are alive, you have a lot to live for, and you are not a mistake. Because of this, you cannot give up. Don't even think about it! There are better options. Your situation may seem desperate right now. You may believe there is no way out. But there is hope as long as you are alive and breathing.

Please don't make the ultimate mistake by committing suicide. Suicide is never the answer. Ever. Suicide is a permanent solution to a temporary problem.

Facing up to a challenging issue is difficult, and you should not tackle it on your own. Now is the time to reach out for help from friends, family members, teachers, or other trusted adults. Let them know you are scared and that you need support. You will be surprised at how many adults will empathize with you and not judge you. They will want to help you and not hurt you. I believe this with absolute certainty. Breathe. Ask for help. It's not easy, but you must do it.

When I am faced with a big decision or a difficult challenge, sometimes I compose a one act play in my mind. I script out how I believe the conversation will go. I imagine that I know exactly what will be said. I often envision a negative outcome, and I work myself into an anxiety-filled frenzy. What I have found, however, is that when I do reach out to a friend, I was usually wrong to have expected a negative response.

Instead, I find that my friends are there to provide support—not harsh judgement—regardless of the circumstances. It's time for you to give your friends and family a chance. Sure, my friends and family don't always say exactly what I want to hear but that doesn't mean I should keep my fears bottled up. I still need to talk, and I still need to ask for help.

I believe that if you reach out, you will find the support you need to keep going. At the very least, your friends and family can steer you to the right resources. There are countless organizations out there designed to help teens navigate challenging life situations. Check out the resource page in this book for ideas.

The bottom line is that you are valuable. Regardless of the reaction you receive from your parents and friends, teachers or community, you matter and you will get through this.

I never heard back from Emily. I never found out the rest of her story. I emailed her a second time, but she didn't respond. I can only hope that I got through to her and that she is okay.

If you are ever faced with a situation that seems hopeless, please remember that there is always a way out, even when you cannot see it. Do not turn to suicide; the only result is darkness. Choose to breathe. Reach out for a lifeline. Somewhere, someone will help you find the light.

Harriet's Heart

Breathe. Take a second. Just breathe.

You've got this.

Reflections

- When faced with the unexpected twists and turns of life, how have you made it through? What did you learn from the situation? Would you handle it in the same manner if presented with the same situation again?

- When you are faced with a tough situation and you feel desperate, who do you turn to for help or support? Would it depend on the situation?

- Suicide is a permanent solution to a temporary problem. How could you help someone who is contemplating suicide take a step back, breathe, and understand the permanent consequences of this action?

CHAPTER TWELVE

YOUR WORDS HAVE POWER

"Harriet, this is Detective Norris from the Knox County Sheriff's Office in Knox County, Indiana. I'm calling to find out if you are harboring a runaway girl from our area."

As the detective asked this question, my heart began beating faster. Me? Harboring a runaway? I only know one person from Indiana, and his name is Kevin.

"Ummm...no, sir. I'm not. Who am I supposed to be harboring?"

"Are you the same Harriet who recently spoke at a conference for the Indiana Association of Student Councils?" he asked.

"Yes, sir. I am."

"Well, I've interviewed Deanna's friends, parents, and teachers, and they all believe she's run away to find you."

The detective went on to say that the presentation I gave to the 1,500 students who attended that particular conference really made an impact on Deanna. Since then, she hadn't stopped talking about me and the difference I had made in her life. She was on her way to find me.

That presentation, two months prior, was in an older gym with very bad acoustics. It had been the closing session of the conference and the students were tired by the time I took the stage. I remember walking away feeling like I should have done better and that my presentation was just okay. I remember wishing that I had connected with the teens more effectively. But evidently, I had struck a positive chord with one of them.

The detective's phone call had shaken me up. I had talked for less than an hour on a remote gym floor. Deanna and I did not even engage in a personal conversation. Yet my words meant so much to her that she took them to heart. She believed that my message had changed her life so significantly that she wanted to personally connect with me. That was sobering and more than a little scary.

I had always known that being a motivational speaker involved more than just a catchy title. After all, I was trying to promote positive change. When I took the stage at Deanna's school, my goal was to use my words to make a difference. But Deanna's reaction had reminded me of the power of words and the responsibility that comes with delivering them.

This powerful experience had occurred only a few years into my speaking career. Before that particular presentation, I was nervous because I was the closing speaker, following two other speakers who were heroes to me. They had both hit oratorical homeruns with the audience, and I was in awe of their talent, creativity, and passion. A few minutes before taking the stage, I had gone into the bathroom and called another speaker friend for support. I expressed concern that no one would like me. His reply was, "Don't be nervous. Be awesome."

Easy for him to say, right? But his words challenged me to focus on my passion and not worry about the audience's reaction. I had a message to give, and it was not about me. It was about the hopes and dreams of our future leaders. And somewhere in the words that I had chosen so carefully, Deanna's life was changed—for better or for worse.

Imagine. If I had that kind of influence in 45 minutes among 1,500 students in a gym with bad sound, just think about the power you can have with friends and family members. You are with them every day, sometimes for eight hours or more. Sometimes, we have no idea that what we say is having a powerful impact on someone's life. Sometimes, we are too afraid to connect with others because we worry about how we will be received. Sometimes we need to grab the microphone and let it FLY! Or as my friend challenged me, we need to trample our nerves so that we can be awesome.

The good news was that Deanna was found safe a few days after the detective's phone call. I never heard from her. But I learned a valuable lesson. My words matter. They matter when I am delivering a formal presentation to a group of students. They matter when I am on the phone, talking with a friend. And they matter when I am face to face with my son.

You may not be a powerful speaker to thousands of people, but you are still capable of influencing the people around you with your words. Sometimes, it's the small conversations that have the most impact on people. It's a few well-placed words of wisdom that can turn someone's day around. Or it's an off-handed comment that we should have kept to ourselves that can be the most hurtful. And sometimes, it's what we don't say—those lost opportunities when we could have offered helpful advice or encouragement but we were too afraid to speak out.

The point is to think before you speak. Use your words for good.

Here are some strategies that can help you harness the power of your words and use them to be a positive influence on the people in your life.

- *Study great people.* Mentoring can be a powerful force and most successful people have had someone who served as a positive influence. Begin by reading about your personal heroes. Follow their rise to success. Who were the people who influenced them? What were the powerful messages that helped them achieve their goals?

- *Take inventory of your personal attributes.* Make a list of your positive qualities. What do your friends and family most admire about you? What skills do you possess? Discover your assets and you will realize which traits can be used to help you become more effective at influencing others.

- *Identify the issues that are holding you back.* Maybe you have some issues that make you reluctant to speak out. Many people feel afraid or shy when faced with the prospect of sharing words and opinions. Some of us are afraid that we will be met with rejection or anger. Believe in yourself and realize that you have the power to make a positive difference.

- *Be unique.* You will never influence the world by trying to imitate everyone else. Be yourself. You might have just what it takes to be an influential voice of encouragement.

- *Be a motivator.* Take a stand for what you believe in. Speak kind words. Be a positive influence. We are often bombarded by negative influences in our world. Be an encouraging voice, and make a difference.

As a motivational speaker, I get to do what I love. I have taken inventory of my strengths and my passions: my voice, my research, my humor, my excitement, my love for young people, my appreciation of parenting. I use all of these things as fuel for what I hope will be an impactful presentation.

And then there are the words. I choose them carefully because I know that I have a big responsibility. The right words are powerful, and they can make a difference.

Harriet's Heart

Some thoughts are better left in your

head.

But thoughtful words can make

someone's day.

Reflections

- If I were to ask you whose words have been the most encouraging to you and whose words have been the most damaging, would you be able to immediately think of a person or persons? Which one was the easiest to remember—positive or negative?

- Why are we careful about what we say to some people but not others? Are our families and close friends sometimes on the receiving end of our harshest comments? If so, why?

- Why do some people bully others who seem to be easy targets? What can we do to be more uplifting and encouraging to each other?

CHAPTER THIRTEEN

YOU ARE VALUABLE

"You saved my life today."

He looked so much like my son. "Excuse me?" I asked.

"What you said in the assembly...you saved my life," repeated Logan. "I wasn't sure if I'd ever feel better, but you let me know that things will keep getting better if I just hold on."

I was running short on time, but I was intrigued by this young man's comments. It was clear that he had something important to say.

"What's going on," I asked. "Why do you say that I saved your life?"

"Well, I'm living with a foster family now. They are awesome, but I'm with them because my mom tried to kill me," Logan explained.

Whoa. My mind was screaming, "WHAT DID YOU

JUST SAY?" I heard the words, but I couldn't truly comprehend them. Maybe he was exaggerating. After all, my mother and I had engaged in some serious fights, especially in my teen years. Parent-child relationships are tough, especially in the adolescent years when both teens and parents are testing new boundaries. But as a mother, I couldn't relate to the concept of actually wanting to kill my child.

"Did you have a bad fight?" I asked.

"Yes and no. When she uses drugs, she loses control," Logan explained. "One day she got really mad about something. The last thing I remember was that she had her legs around my neck choking me. I couldn't get away and she was screaming, 'I never wanted you anyway and my life would be better if I just got rid of you right now!' The police came, and I ended up in the hospital. I was checked out by a doctor, and for the most part, I was fine. I haven't been home since."

As someone who focuses on youth advocacy in much of my work, I know that the statistics regarding child abuse are startling. I also know that the victims of abuse aren't always small children. In fact, thousands of teens are abused every year. The National Children's Alliance served 315,806 victims of child abuse in 2014. Of these victims, 81,025 were between the ages of 13 and 18.[1]

As I looked at Logan, it occurred to me that he was

[1]NCA National Statistics - Statistical Report 2014. National Children's Alliance.
http://www.nationalchildrensalliance.org/sites/default/files/download-files/2014NationalAnnual_0.pdf

not just a statistic. He was real. As he related the incident, I became sure of two things. First, Logan had been abused before and this type of home life had become "normal" for him. Secondly, he was in pain. His comments revealed how desperate he was for a strong support system.

This was one of those times when a career composed of motivating and inspiring young people was gratifying and sobering at the same time. I am always happy to be there for kids like Logan who need some extra inspiration. But my heart breaks when I hear about the extreme difficulties that so many young people are facing.

I zeroed in on a key question. "Tell me about your situation now. How are you doing?"

His face yielded a slight smile. "I have a great foster family. They love me. They take me to church and have taught me about God. They've let me know that this is not my fault, no matter what my mom said or did. They have shown me that I am loved by God and I am His child. I am not a mistake. I'm here for a purpose. I just have to figure out what that purpose is."

I challenged him. "What do you think your purpose might be?"

"As I listened to you, I knew that what I want to do is help kids who are going through a tough time at home realize how valuable they are," he replied.

I shook my head in amazement. "You got all of that from my program?"

He nodded. "Yeah, I did. You helped me by the way you explained life. You gave me hope. I needed to hear it because today has been a really bad day, and I was thinking that this is so embarrassing living the life I have. Sometimes, I can't handle it. Thanks for letting me know that I can."

I amplified my statements. "We have to get through the tough times to really appreciate the good times. And that's why we have to have friends on our side. That's why we have to have people we can reach out to— people who will lift us up when we are down or when we need help. That's why we can't keep our problems to ourselves and we have to let people in. Many times, we think we are the only ones with a certain problem when, in reality, others are hurting in similar ways."

In Logan's case, he was already learning about the importance of reaching out to caring individuals. He was feeling loved by an emotionally healthy family, and he was feeling loved by God. He was learning that he mattered and that he could have a great life.

But while Logan was on the right track, there are many kids suffering from abusive situations who haven't yet realized that they deserve to be loved. There are many teens living in homes where there is constant fighting, unhappiness, or abuse. Sometimes, these kids isolate themselves or live in denial by pretending that their homes are normal so they won't be embarrassed by their dysfunctional families. They walk around in shame, not realizing that there are other young people suffering through similar situations.

By keeping their pain to themselves, they are trapped in a downward spiral until finally something devastating happens to them. Many times, they become vulnerable to serious dangers including drug abuse, alcohol addiction, or suicide. These tragedies happen every day.

I am not a psychologist, but common sense tells me

that when someone is made to feel worthless, then he or she begins to act out in ways that support those beliefs. In Logan's case, moving into a nurturing foster home halted the destructive process. He received the validation he needed to know that he was a valuable person. He was able to see that he was not the problem, and it cleared his mind and heart to begin making healthy changes and even to make a plan for a positive future.

Everyone wants to feel loved and accepted. Everyone. Even you.

So when you see someone who is obviously hurting, reach out to him or her. You don't have to save this person's life. You probably couldn't even if you tried. But you can let your friend know that he or she is valuable and that there is hope. More importantly, you can help your friend find special resources that can provide extra help. I have included some in the back of this book to give you a head start. Even with the best intentions and hours of conversation, you simply don't have the skills of a trained professional. The best thing you can do is to make sure your friend is in a safe place and has access to someone who is qualified to help.

Because if you don't step in, maybe no one else will either. And for someone who is hurting, knowing that someone cares might be the key to survival.

Harriet's Heart

Someone, somewhere thinks you are

awesome.

Find them!

Reflections

- Have you kept a secret because of fear of embarrassment, shame, or worry about punishment if you say too much?

- If you are concerned that a friend is in a negative or hurtful situation but they have asked you not to discuss it with anyone, how could you be a friend and help that person get the support they need? Is there a trusted adult or professional that you could reach out to?

- Have you ever been surprised to learn someone's true story? Would some of your friends be surprised to learn your story?

CHAPTER FOURTEEN

ENCOURAGEMENT FOR EVERYONE

"I don't have anything to write about," said Tori.

I had just finished explaining a writing activity to more than 100 middle level and high school students. Tori was obviously one of the younger students in attendance, and I thought some ideas might help her get started on the assignment. "The activity is to write about a challenge you are having that others could help you with; this could be about grades, something going on at home, some troubles with a friend, or maybe an issue about life in general," I said.

"But that's what I mean. I don't have anything to write. I don't have any problems. My family is good and so are my friends. I make good grades. I don't know what to write about."

Wow. No problems or issues at all? I wanted her life.

"The idea is for you to share about something you need

help with and for others to offer helpful solutions or words of encouragement. If you have absolutely no problems or issues at all, then maybe you can think of a problem one of your friends is having," I suggested.

She shook her head. "No. They are happy, too. I don't know what you want me to do."

I was trapped in Pleasantville, and she was the mayor. "Okay. What if you write down some words of encouragement in response to the issues that others are sharing? Sound good?" She nodded and returned to her place in the group.

I wondered if Tori really didn't have any issues or if she was just unwilling to share them. I wasn't asking her or anyone else to share their deep, dark secrets, but I thought that everyone would have a challenge to write about. As I watched Tori happily writing words of encouragement on other people's papers, it occurred to me that Tori was more like me than I cared to admit. It is easier for me to focus on other people's issues. That way, I don't have to acknowledge my own stuff.

I am rarely excited about analyzing myself. Those personality quizzes in magazines are difficult for me to complete. When I am asked a lot of questions about how I feel, what makes me happy, or my life's goals, I always want to add another choice to the list of options. I want a box that says, "I don't know."

When it comes to personal conversations, I prefer to keep it on the surface. Some might say I like to be in control. I probably wouldn't argue that point. What if I did focus on me and I discovered emotions other than happiness? That would ruin my day. The only thing worse than stumbling upon an abyss is to fall into it. What if I really had to think about Harriet versus the world? That would be a lot tougher than just focusing on the positives. What if I really thought about what I wanted and when I came up with some answers, I realized that I needed other people to help me get where I wanted to go? That would be tough, too, because I like to do things on my own.

We are living in a culture that promotes independence, authority, and control. Many of us have a natural tendency to hold on to our power and stay in charge. Much of our presence in today's world actually comes in the form of selfies—mini snapshots that highlight only our best features. We display a public persona but guard our true identities. We keep the deep knowledge about ourselves and our emotions private. But when we block everyone out and don't share our feelings, there can be consequences. We can become lonely, depressed, isolated, and confused. We might start to wonder who we really are.

In a famous poem, John Donne writes:

No man is an island,
Entire of itself,
Every man is a piece of the continent,
A part of the main.

Over time, I have developed an appreciation for this author's sentiments. As much as we would like to hide from others and pretend that we are okay by ourselves, we thrive when we are connected. Yet many of us push people away or don't let others get to know who we really are because we are afraid of being rejected. I have learned that isolation is not healthy. When we don't share our thoughts and feelings with the people close to us, we end up believing that we are the only one who is struggling. We need to know that we are more alike than we are different. We all face challenges from time to time.

Here are some encouraging life lessons that might help you deal with the obstacles in your life.

- *Everyone has times of despair.* We all experience a wide range of emotions— happiness, sadness, anger, fear, confusion, worry. Acknowledge your feelings. Don't be afraid to be imperfect. You were not designed to be happy 100 percent of the time. Life is a wild ride. Hang on.

- *Realize that whatever emotion you are experiencing is temporary.* If you are sad, realize that this time of grief will pass. You are liquid mercury constantly changing emotional shape from moment to moment. If you are in panic mode or are feeling afraid, take some steps to move past these feelings. In the back of this book is a resource page with names of organizations that can help. Even in times of happiness, the feeling will pass. It may be difficult, but let it go. Go with the flow and acknowledge that emotions are always changing.

- *Ask close friends for help.* Don't ask everyone you know for their opinion—just a few, trusted friends. Consider their advice and take time to think about it. Add your own thoughts to the mix and then decide what to do. Under no circumstance should you do what someone says just to make them happy. When you do this and you are not 100 percent happy with this decision, the person who loses in the end is you. Trust your gut. It doesn't lie.

- *Stay present.* It's hard to see it at the time, but our most difficult situations can end up providing valuable life lessons. Deal with what is happening right now. Stop worrying about what will happen days, weeks, months, or even years from now. Make decisions that will benefit your life today. Make responsible decisions that you have taken the time to really think about; guard against spontaneous choices that might be reckless or could create more trouble down the line.

- *Take ACTION!* It is completely acceptable to lie in your bed, sleep, and do nothing for a few days. But after a few days, get up, take a shower, and do something. Call a friend, exercise, and create an action plan to get your life in order. Be intentional. Realize that nothing will get better if you don't take action.

I would love to live in a world where life is always happy and there are no worries. I can't. Neither can you or anyone else. So don't look at challenges as insurmountable. See them as opportunities to learn about life. As you experience life, get to know yourself. Be on the lookout for someone who needs encouragement. Send them a thoughtful note or speak to them with well-chosen words. And while you're at it, don't forget to encourage yourself. You deserve it. We all do.

Harriet's Heart

Things may not be great in your life

right now.

Hang on! Your time is coming.

Reflections

- Are you able to examine your life and weigh both the positive and negative parts, or are you content to describe your life as "it's all good"?

- How does it make you feel when you are sharing a concern and people say, "Be glad you don't have to deal with this. . . ."? Should we compare our problems to things other people are facing? How can you validate what others are feeling?

- How can you be encouraging to your friends or others you come in contact with—even if it's just a small gesture?

CHAPTER FIFTEEN

INVISIBLE

"I'm invisible after 3 o'clock." The petite girl with dark brown eyes spoke quietly as she stared down at the floor.

"What do you mean you are invisible after 3 o'clock?" I asked.

Keisha looked up at me and replied, "You know how you said that everyone should feel a part of this school and get involved? Well, I am. I have friends. I'm in chorus, and people seem to like me there. Everything is fine during the school day. But as soon as 3 o'clock hits and school is out, I'm invisible. I have no friends. I don't understand why. I'm never invited to a friend's house or a party; like I've never been to a party. No one will come over to my house. I don't get it. It's been this way since seventh grade. Now, I'm a senior. I hate my life, and in two months, it will be time for graduation. I don't want to hear about all the grad parties because I know I won't be invited to any."

I knew that there was no way this girl's life was going to change in two months. A pattern had been established. For six years, she had been forgotten about after school. Six years. There was definitely something going on that I didn't know about, and I was not going to be able to help Keisha solve this problem in a short amount of time.

"Okay. Here's the deal. Your life is not going to change until you leave this school. I have no idea what is wrong and why you are excluded. I do know it should not be this way, and I am so sorry. I wish that I could wave a magic wand and your friends would start inviting you to parties, but I can't. Even if I could, you would still carry some scars from the past six years. You might not even be able to enjoy the parties because you'd wonder why your friends have been excluding you from everything. Your exclusion doesn't make sense, and you will probably never be able to figure it all out. But here is the good news. In two short months, you will graduate and move on to the next chapter of your life. What are you planning to do after high school?"

Keisha explained that she would be attending college in a town about two hours away. "Perfect," I said. "Your new life is about to begin. You will be able to start over, make new friends, and no one will know what happened during these difficult years. I promise things will be different. Invisible Keisha will become visible, and life will be better. College is a completely different environment. There are so many new opportunities, groups, and interesting ways to meet people. But you cannot sit back and expect people to come to you. Go to the student union and look for ways to get involved. Search for volunteer opportunities, clubs, and group events. Explore your interests. Discover new ventures. Look for healthy places where you can find a place to belong.

College is the perfect opportunity to rediscover yourself and fine tune your skills. If you were shy at this school, work on expanding your social skills. Step out of your comfort zone, and be more outgoing. You can think of it this way. Every, single freshman is coming from a new city, maybe even a new country. Everyone is nervous about finding a place to belong. No one wants be invisible, but at the same time, everyone will be trying to blend in. You know what it feels like to be invisible, so be on the lookout for someone you can connect with.

And when this year's senior parties begin here at your high school and you start to feel alone, remember that this time will pass. It won't make the moments feel any better, but it will give you something to look forward to. During the graduation ceremony when you walk across that stage and receive your diploma, don't look back. Get on with your life and do your thing. Got it?" Keisha managed a tentative nod. She wasn't 100 percent happy when she headed off to her fifth period class, but she was doing better.

As the principal approached me, I asked about Keisha and mentioned that she was feeling isolated after school. He seemed surprised when I relayed what she'd just told me. "Really? I had no idea. She's always with a group of students. She's involved in chorus, and she's never been the subject of any reported issues. This is really interesting. I'll see what I can do to help her."

While the principal was genuinely interested in helping Keisha, there were only two months left in her high school years. Two months. Yet, she'd been at this school for four years, and seemingly, no one had suspected any problems. No one had reported to the principal that this girl seemed lonely or forgotten—ever. Was I really the only person that Keisha had spoken to about this issue since it began in seventh grade? Was what she said really true? Was she really invisible after 3 o'clock?

I seriously doubted that Keisha magically became invisible when the dismissal bell rang. But it was clear that something was going on. There were some details that made her "no fun" after school, and the fact that not one person cared enough or maybe even knew enough about this girl's situation to notice really bothered me. Whose fault was it? I could easily charge into the student leadership class and blast them for not making sure that Keisha was happy on campus. But wait—she was happy during the day. It was after school when the problems began. Was it beyond Keisha's control? Was it a family issue? Did other parents not want their children to associate with her? I will never know, but what I do know is that one very confused student went through most of middle school and high school feeling alone.

Life can be one chaotic mass of contradiction and confusion. There will always be situations that we just can't figure out. We might feel a connection with a certain group, and then as soon as we feel like we belong, something happens and we are alone again. And then there are those times when we would actually prefer to be invisible. Why is it that at those times— when we'd rather blend into the scenery—everyone seems to be watching us, but when we want to be noticed, no one does?

So what do you during those times when you'd like to feel more connected? You have to survive and get through it. Try looking at your situation through a different lens. Maybe your school friends are just that—friends at school. Maybe you can establish deeper connections through a youth-oriented club outside of school. Look for opportunities to become involved in a youth group at your church, synagogue, or community center. Volunteer to be a mentor for younger students. Do anything that keeps you moving and motivates your brain to think positive thoughts.

It's easy when you feel invisible to act invisible. Don't. You don't have to be in the spotlight, but make yourself noticed. Talk to people, and be conscious of how you interact with others. If you are always sitting down when groups of people are around, start standing up. If you are always standing with your arms crossed in front of you, open your arms and put them on your hips, or put one hand on your hip and let one arm hang down. Don't close yourself off from others with your words or your actions! Look at people with a smile on your face—not a big, scary, Joker-like smile—but a friendly smile that shows people you are approachable. Who knows? Your social experiment might just be the most awkward thing ever, or it could help you make new friends and let people see that you are a really fun person to be around. And remember that not all attention is positive. Be yourself, make good choices, and use common sense.

Feeling invisible is never fun. We all have times when we feel overlooked or left out. Yep, we all do.

When you have those times, even if they feel like they will never, ever end, you must hold on to the hope that things will get better. Those times will end, and tomorrow—or two months from now—you will be like Keisha, on the verge of new adventures and opportunities if you are willing to take the first step and open the door to your future.

No one remains invisible forever.

Harriet's Heart

I am not in control of what other

people do to me.

I am in control of what I do to me.

Reflections

- Have you ever had a time when you felt invisible or alone?

- What did you do to become a part of the group or at least get acknowledged?

- What are some ways you can help yourself from feeling invisible in the future?

EPILOGUE

When I was in high school, it wasn't easy to connect with people outside of my community. Now, with access to the Internet and the touch of a button, teens can connect with anyone in any corner of the world. But even with so much online access, many teens still feel isolated, alone, and misunderstood—just like I did when I was their age. I wonder if it might be even more difficult today, because in this age of online communications, many teens aren't taking the time to actually talk to their friends and build healthy relationships outside of the impersonal constraints of cyberspace.

Through the true stories in this book, I wanted to provide a glimpse into some of the challenging issues facing today's teens. Many of their concerns are the same concerns that my friends and I shared when we were in high school. I wanted you to understand that many teens are searching for a sense of self, a place to belong, and someone—anyone—who can help them feel better. I believe this is why teens sometimes make poor choices. If there is someone out there who gives the appearance of caring, they will gravitate towards that person, even if it's not in their best interests.

I wanted you to know that there are teens out there who are just like you. And though we all don't wrestle with the exact same problems, we all struggle with something. This is why we have to take care of each other. People are good at hiding their emotions. It might not be easy to see the pain or sadness that a friend, family member, or an acquaintance is experiencing. But we need to be aware.

Be there for each other. Lift each other up. You never know who might need you the most.

RESOURCES FOR TEENS

2-1-1 is a free and confidential service provided by the United Way that helps people across North America find the resources and help they need. From crisis and emergency, to jobs and support, someone is available 24 hours a day, 7 days a week.

www.call211.org

The Date Safe Project provides powerful and trustworthy guidance for addressing relationships, intimacy, sexual decision-making, and sexual assault. You'll find out how to make relationships more fun, romantic, and respectful.

www.DateSafeProject.org

#iCANHELP is a nationally recognized public charity that works with students, parents, and teachers to create a safe internet and positive social media connections.

www.iCanHelpDeleteNegativity.org

loveisrepect strives to empower youth and provides support and strategies for the prevention and end of dating abuse.

www.loveisrespect.org
Call 1-866-331-9474
Text loveis to 22522

National Children's Alliance helps local communities serve the victims of child abuse.

www.NationalChildrensAlliance.org
Call 1-202-548-0090

National Eating Disorders Association (NEDA) supports individuals and families affected by eating disorders.

www.NationalEatingDisorders.org
Call 1-800-931-2237

National Suicide Prevention Lifeline. No matter what problems you are having, no matter what time of day or night, someone is available to talk.

www.SuicidePreventionLifeline.org
Call: 1-800-273-TALK (8255)

It's tough to be a teen. *JustBeU* is a comprehensive, easy-to-use curriculum that teaches girls how to navigate the adolescent years with courage, overcome their fears, and realize their true worth.

Through a series of relevant lesson plans, Just Be U is designed to reach girls where they are with topics that matter. Get the curriculum. Implement the lessons. Watch girls discover the real "U" inside each of them.

Check out some of the topics:

- Body Image
- Strengths and Weaknesses
- Stereotypes and the Media
- Healthy Relationships
- Finding Your Purpose
- Bullying
- Developing Your Voice
- Owning Your Power
- Creating Your Future

Go to www.justbeu.com to learn more.

TELL YOUR STORY

Ashlyn Schroyer, Landon Schmidt, Harriet Turk, Seth McKay, and Aedan McKay

Please visit www.transparenthearts.com and share your views about the book and the stories. What story affected you the most and why? What topics would you like to see featured in an upcoming book?

If you'd like to tell Harriet your story, there's a special place to do so on the website. We'd love to hear from you.

The site will also include additional resources and updates just for you.

ABOUT THE AUTHOR

For more than 25 years, Harriet Turk has been inspiring teens and adults to discover their true identities and pursue a life of substance. She has worked as a probation officer, youth programs coordinator, flight attendant, pharmaceutical sales rep, college-level instructor, and nationally-known professional speaker, trainer, and consultant. Harriet is also a mom, friend, sister, and daughter.

When she was a teen, Harriet struggled with her own identity crisis. She fell into the trap of feeling like she had to be perfect. Her life experiences have taught her that success and happiness come from celebrating who you are and pursuing a life that honors your strengths and abilities.

Because Harriet's stories and experiences come from real life, her message is authentic, relatable, and compelling.

To learn more about Harriet and her motivational programs for teens and adults or to book Harriet for your next event, go to:
www.harrietturk.com
www.thisaintyodream.com

Follow Harriet on instagram/twitter/fb: harrietturk

Made in the USA
Columbia, SC
22 January 2019